HOT WHEELS: The Newest Stock Car Stars

TRADITION BOOKS™
EXCELSIOR, MINNESOTA

BY BOB WOODS

Published by **Tradition Books**™ and distributed to the
school and library market by **The Child's World**®
P.O. Box 326
Chanhassen, MN 55317-0326
800/599-READ
http://www.childsworld.com

Photo Credits
Cover and title page: Allsport/Jonathan Ferrey
Allsport: 16 (Jonathan Ferrey); 19 (Chris Stanford); 22 (David Taylor)
AP/Wide World: 9, 10, 11, 17, 18, 21, 27, 28, 29
Sports Gallery: 5 (Brian Spurlock); 7, 24 (Al Messerschmidt); 13, 14 (Tom Riles);
26 (Joe Robbins)

Book production by Shoreline Publishing Group, LLC
Art direction and design by The Design Lab

Library of Congress Cataloging-in-Publication Data

Woods, Bob.
  Hot wheels : the newest stock car stars / by Bob Woods.
     p. cm. — (The world of NASCAR series)
Includes bibliographical references and index.
  ISBN 1-59187-006-2 (lib. bdg. : alk. paper)
  1. Automobile racing drivers—United States—Biography—Juvenile literature. 2. Stock
car racing—United States—Juvenile literature. [1. Automobile racing drivers. 2. Stock
car racing.] I. Title. II. Series.
  GV1032.A1 W67 2002
  796.72'092'2—dc21   2002004645

Printed in the United States of America.

HOT WHEELS

Table of Contents

4 **Introduction:** Hot Wheels

6 **Chapter One:** Kevin Harvick: A Season to Remember

12 **Chapter Two:** Dale Earnhardt Jr.: The Son Also Rises

19 **Chapter Three:** Casey Atwood: Young and Talented

25 **Chapter Four:** Shawna Robinson: Move Over, Guys!

30 Glossary

31 For More Information about NASCAR's Rising Stars

32 Index

INTRODUCTION

Hot Wheels

T he National Association for **Stock Car** Auto Racing, or **NASCAR,** was founded in 1948. Car owner and former driver William "Big Bill" France started the organization in Daytona Beach, Florida. Today, NASCAR is one of the most popular sports in the world. The main reason is the daredevil drivers who get behind the wheels of their brightly colored cars on race day.

Every season, new drivers come and go. Some become popular superstars, others simply fade away. The biggest names in NASCAR history—from Junior Johnson and Richard Petty to Dale Jarrett and Jeff Gordon—started racing when they were young. All of them eventually worked their way to the top. As in any sport, you have to pay your dues before you reach the highest level.

In NASCAR, that level is the **Winston Cup Series.**
Hot Wheels introduces you to four of the hottest young
Winston Cup drivers. They're the next generation of stars—if
all goes well.

Meet Kevin Harvick. In 2001, he was both the Winston
Cup Rookie of the Year and the **Busch Series** champion.
Dale Earnhardt Jr. is one of many sons of famous drivers.
What makes the story of "Little E" a bit sad was the tragic
death of Dale Earnhardt Sr. in 2001. Casey Atwood has never
let his young age keep him from becoming a winning driver.
Shawna Robinson is trying to become one of the few women
to break into the Winston Cup ranks.

Keep an eye on this foursome. You're likely to find them
on **Victory Lane** for years to come.

Dale Earnhardt Jr. follows in the tire tracks of his
seven-time NASCAR champion father Dale.

CHAPTER ONE

Kevin Harvick: A Season to Remember

About the only thing Kevin Harvick didn't win in 2001 was the lottery. Kevin is just 26 years old, a friendly young driver from Bakersfield, California. He has a smile as wide as the beaches of Daytona and was named 2001 NASCAR Winston Cup Rookie of the Year. He also won the championship in NASCAR's Busch Series, stock car racing's top "minor league" circuit.

In 2001, Harvick won two Winston Cup races and five Busch races. He earned a total of $4.6 million from races. He also won the hand of DeLana Linville. Kevin and DeLana were married in Las Vegas in February. It was an amazing year in his young life. He had been racing toward it from his earliest days.

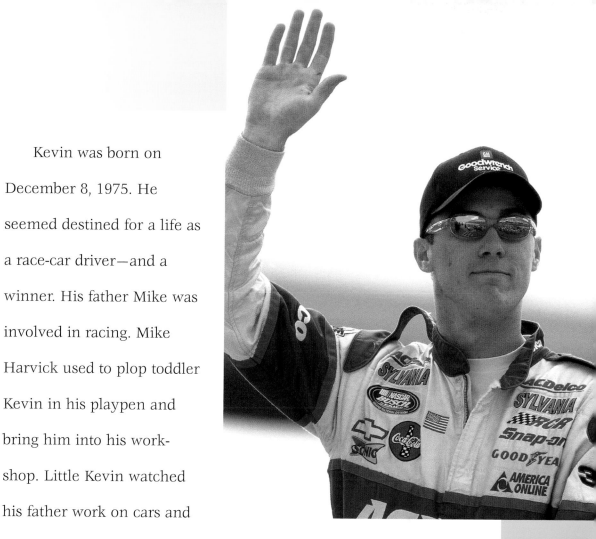

Kevin was born on December 8, 1975. He seemed destined for a life as a race-car driver—and a winner. His father Mike was involved in racing. Mike Harvick used to plop toddler Kevin in his playpen and bring him into his workshop. Little Kevin watched his father work on cars and engines. When Kevin finished kindergarten, his parents rewarded him with his very own **go-kart.**

"My dad had a lot to do with my start in racing," Kevin says. "As a hobby, he's been working on cars since 1977. He was even a **crew chief** for a regional **race team** for a couple of years. He has always worked on stock cars. That's how we got the money for me to race go-karts."

Kevin Harvick has been greeted with success at every level of racing he has tried.

Kevin was a natural behind the wheel of a go-kart. He also was a big-time winner even then. In 10 years on the circuit, he captured seven National Championships and a pair of Grand National Championships. By the time he got to high school, though, Kevin was ready to race real cars. In 1992, he started competing in the Featherlite Southwest Series, a regional NASCAR division. In 1995, his first full season, he was named Rookie of the Year.

Kevin enrolled at Bakersfield Junior College, where he studied architecture. What he really wanted to do, however, was race. In 1997, he made a tough decision. He left college to devote himself full-time to the career he really loved. "Racing is something I've wanted to do my whole life," he explains. "I chose racing, and I've never looked back."

In 1998, Kevin continued his winning ways. He took the **checkered flag** in five races in NASCAR's Winston West Series. Those victories helped him earn the driver's championship. Then he hooked on briefly with the Craftsman Truck

Series, just long enough to impress Richard Childress. This well-known car owner invited Kevin to drive one of his racers in the Busch Series in 2000. Kevin won there, too, and was named Rookie of the Year.

Kevin planned to race the Busch circuit again in 2001. However, in February, superstar Dale Earnhardt was killed in a crash at the Daytona 500. Childress needed a new driver for that car. He chose Kevin.

They changed the color of Earnhardt's car from black to white. They also changed Earnhardt's famous number 3 to number 29. The young former go-kart champion was in the most famous seat in stock car racing. He quickly lived up to his potential. In just his third start, at the Cracker Barrel 500 in

Kevin got his first taste of speed in small, gas-powered go-karts like these.

Atlanta, Kevin won. No other NASCAR driver since 1972 had gained a victory so quickly.

He crossed the finish line first again in July, at the Tropicana 400 in Chicago. By season's end in November, Kevin had notched six top-five finishes. He also was in the top 10 in 16 races. His success made him the Winston Cup's top rookie. Amazingly, he also competed in the Busch Series every week-end. Instead of racing just once a week, he often raced twice. In all, he was in 69 races in 2001. He is the only NASCAR driver ever to race full-time in both series.

"This was just a dream season," said an exhausted but happy Kevin at the Busch awards banquet. He announced that he planned to race only in Winston Cup events in 2002. He can probably plan, too, on a long career of winning more races and championships.

Kevin drove this car in the Busch Series while also competing in Winston Cup races.

A FANTASTIC FINISH

Kevin Harvick's first Winston Cup victory will go down as one of NASCAR's most thrilling races ever. Kevin was running in the middle of the pack for most of the Cracker Barrel 500 in Atlanta. Then, with less than 10 laps to go, Kevin surged ahead. He passed the leader, Jeff Gordon. That set off a furious finish.

The race came down to the final two nail-biting laps. Kevin found himself in a pack of five cars, speeding along door-to-door, bumper-to-bumper. He slid by Dale Jarrett and Jerry Nadeau. Then Dale Earnhardt Jr. suffered a tire problem. That left just Kevin, the raw rookie, and Jeff, the three-time Winston Cup championship winner.

They streaked side-by-side to the checkered flag. Kevin barely won—by a mere six tenths of a second! "I think somebody was watching over us today," said an emotional Kevin following the race. Of course, he was talking about the Intimidator, Dale Earnhardt Sr., who only a few weeks earlier was killed in the Daytona 500. Kevin had taken over Dale's ride on owner Richard Childress' team. He also was driving the same car in which Earnhardt had won the same race the year before—in a photo finish.

Kevin celebrates a win in Tennessee in the Busch Series, getting ready to make the jump to Winston Cup.

C H A P T E R   T W O

Dale Earnhardt Jr.: The Son Also Rises

S tock car racing history is filled with famous families of drivers: fathers, sons, and brothers. The Flocks, the Pettys, the Jarretts, the Allisons, and the Waltrips are just a few of those families. Another of the most famous is the Earnhardts.

In 1999, when Dale Earnhardt Jr. started Winston Cup racing, he knew he had big shoes to fill. Until two years later, he had no idea just how big. Dale's famous father, Dale Sr., was known as the "the Intimidator." Dale Jr. was following behind one of NASCAR's biggest stars.

Dale Jr., or "Little E," had already earned a name for himself before the 2001 Winston Cup season. Dale Jr. was

also the grandson of early stock car racing legend Ralph Earnhardt. The young driver truly had driving skills in his blood. He was around fast cars and racetracks from the moment he was born in North Carolina in 1974. Dale Jr. turned pro at age 17. He started out in NASCAR's Street Stock division. His car was a 1978 Monte Carlo that he co-owned with his older half-brother, Kerry.

It didn't take long before Little E was carrying on the family tradition. Within two years, he worked his way up to the NASCAR **Late Model** Stock division. In 1996, only 21 years old, he joined the Busch Series. In his first race, he

Two Dales: The late Dale Earnhardt was an inspiration and a teacher for his son Dale (right).

finished 14th, not bad for a rookie. The following year, he ran in eight Busch races, posting one top-10 finish.

By 1998, he was a member of his father's prestigious racing team, Dale Earnhardt Inc. (DEI). That year Little E was a full-time driver on the Busch circuit. His career really shifted into high gear. Driving an AC Delco-sponsored car, he posted his first win at the Texas Motor Speedway in April. He went on to take

For some special races, Dale Jr. climbs into his father's famous No. 3 car.

six more checkered flags that season. By the end of the year,
he had won the Busch Series driver's championship. He
became the first third-generation NASCAR driver to win a
series title.

Little E started slowly at the beginning of the 1999 season. He soon got back on the winning track. He racked up a
total of six victories on the season. At one point, he won an
incredible three races in a row. Along with earning another
driver's championship, Little E won a Busch Series season-
record $1,680,598.

Now the son was ready to join his father on the Winston
Cup circuit. Dale Jr. got five races under his belt in 1999. He
insisted he was ready to move up to full-time in 2000. In his
new Winston Cup car, Little E showed respect for his rich
racing ancestry. He painted No. 8 on the doors and hood of
his Chevrolet Monte Carlo. That was the number of his
grandfather, the great racer Ralph Earnhardt.

Little E started 34 Winston Cup races that year, winning

twice. He also had three top-five finishes and five top-10s. He barely missed out on winning Rookie of the Year honors. However, he still made NASCAR history. Competing with him in the Pepsi 400 at Michigan International Speedway were both Dale Sr. and Little E's brother Kerry. The event marked just the second time in NASCAR history that a father and two sons raced together.

Like every Winston Cup season, the 2001 season opened with the traditional Daytona 500. On the last lap, Little E was in second place, right behind DEI teammate Michael Waltrip.

LIKE FATHER, LIKE SON

When he arrived at Daytona International Speedway for the 2001 Pepsi 400 in July, Dale Earnhardt Jr. was filled with emotion. It was his first time back at the track where Dale Sr., one of the most beloved drivers ever, had died on the last lap of NASCAR's season-opening Daytona 500. At the time, the elder Earnhardt was running third behind Michael Waltrip and Little E. All three drivers were teammates on owner Richard Childress' team.

Now, five months later, Waltrip and Earnhardt Jr. were again first and second on the last lap. This time, however, Little E crossed the finish line first. He won by the tiny margin of only .123 seconds. In an eerie coincidence, Dale Sr. had won a race at Daytona exactly 11 years earlier.

"He was with me tonight," Little E said later. He told reporters how he had felt his father's winning spirit. "I dedicate this win to him. I mean, there isn't anybody else I could dedicate it to who would mean more to me."

Dale's hard-charging style works just as well on road courses, as here at Sears Point (left). The way Dale Jr. is going, he had better get used to lifting trophies like this one from the Pepsi 400 (above).

Waltrip would eventually win the race.

Just behind Dale Jr., however, was Dale Sr. As the cars screamed toward the finish line, Dale Sr. suddenly collided with Sterling Marlin. The elder Earnhardt's car crashed head-on into the wall. The Intimidator, Little E's dad, died instantly. The entire racing world was stunned. Little E, of course, was affected most of all. He knew, however, that his dad would want him to keep racing.

Five months later, Little E returned to Daytona for the Pepsi 400. In sixth place with six laps to go, he stormed to victory. The win came exactly 11 years to the day after Dale Sr. won his first race at the Daytona International Speedway. "I don't really think about carrying on the family racing name," says Little E, who would win two more races in 2001. "I'm just so proud of my family." No doubt, the feeling is mutual.

A shocked and sad Dale Jr. leaves the hospital after hearing the terrible news about his father in 2001.

CHAPTER THREE

Casey Atwood: Young and Talented

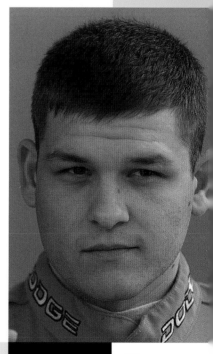

asey Atwood has never let his age stand in the way. He started out racing go-karts when he was 10 years old and moved up to stock cars at 15. When he was just 17, he was already making NASCAR history in the Busch Series. In 2000, the bright-eyed daredevil from Nashville made it to the top: the Winston Cup Series. Casey was just 20 years old. He entered three races that season, then joined the circuit full-time in 2001.

Born on August 25, 1980, Casey grew up outside of Nashville, in the suburb of Antioch, Tennessee. He took to go-kart racing like a fish to water. Starting out in the World Karting Association circuit, he won two

Casey may have a young face, but he is a veteran
driver with a nose for the lead.

championships. He also captured three straight Tennessee State Karting titles.

At 15, a lot of Casey's friends were busy playing baseball, football, and video games. Casey, however, could be found at the Highland Rim Speedway north of Nashville racing stock cars. It didn't take long for him to catch the fans' attention. Before he turned 16, Casey zoomed to more than a dozen victories.

Still, he couldn't stay put. Casey's next step up was the 0.5-mile (0.8-kilometer) Nashville Speedway. At 16, he won 1996 Rookie of the Year honors in the Late Model Stock Car division. Later that year, he demonstrated his driving versatility by driving in a Craftsman Truck Series race.

Casey made his debut in the NASCAR Busch Series in 1998. On the Fourth of July, he won the 1999 DieHard 250 in Milwaukee. At 18 years, 10 months, and nine days old, Casey became the youngest driver ever to win a Busch event.

He won again on September 25, taking the MBNA Gold 200 at Dover Down International Speedway. His breakout

Like many young drivers today, Casey got his start in racing on go-karts like these.

season also featured five top-5 and nine top-10 finishes.
Although still a pup by NASCAR standards, he proved he
was worthy of a Winston Cup ride.

Casey's Winston Cup baptism came in September 2000,
in the Chevrolet Monte Carlo 400. Casey didn't enjoy as much
instant success in Winston Cup as he had in lower NASCAR
divisions. Few experts, however, doubt Casey is a star in the
making.

He was already a fan favorite from his Busch days. He gave
new fans another thrill at the 2001 Pennzoil Freedom 400 in

Casey started out in the Busch Series, driving this
No. 27 car.

HOT TRAINING WHEELS

Just as many major league baseball players start out in Little League, plenty of NASCAR drivers grow up racing go-karts. Casey Atwood, Ricky Rudd, and Tony Stewart are just three such star racers. Atwood started when he was 10, but you only have to be 8 years old to enter some races.

Go-karts are simple and inexpensive. They are made basically of a sturdy chassis and a lawnmower engine. However, they are serious racing machines. The engines range from 5 to 40 horsepower, depending on the level of competition. Go-karts can weigh up to about 300 pounds and reach speeds up to 120 miles per hour (200 kilometers per hour).

Races are held on both oval and twisty road courses. The World Karting Association, formed in 1971, organizes most official go-kart races in the U.S. They are held nearly every weekend all across the country. They even race go-karts at the famous Daytona International Speedway in Florida.

For more information about go-kart racing, check out the association's website at *http://www.worldkarting.com*. You can also write to them at 6051 Victory Lane, Concord, NC 28027. Who knows? Maybe you're the next Casey Atwood?

It was a long road from go-karts to the Winston Cup series, but Casey Atwood made the trip.

Miami. He finished in third place, his best finish. Actually, he appeared well on his way to winning the race when he made a rookie mistake. Veteran drivers Bill Elliott and Michael Waltrip passed him and finished first and second. Casey will take the lessons he learned in those races into his future as a top driver.

In his first full Winston Cup season, Casey drove the No. 19 Dodge owned by Ray Evernham. That famous owner also had superstar Jeff Gordon on his team. Casey recorded three top-10 finishes. Thanks to strong performances at the end of the season, Casey was third in the Rookie of the Year standings. Still just 21, he showed guts, determination and loads of driving skill.

Before the 2002 season, Casey was switched to Evernham's Ultra Motorsports team. His car got a new NASCAR sponsor, Sirius Satellite Radio. Casey hopped into the No. 7 Dodge Intrepid R/T. "I'm anxiously looking forward to the Daytona 500," he said when the announcement was made in January. At least he wasn't going to grow old waiting.

CHAPTER FOUR

Shawna Robinson:
Move Over, Guys!

There have been only a handful of women drivers in NASCAR since it was founded by Big Bill France in 1948. Shawna Robinson has a chance to become the most successful female driver ever.

Shawna was 37 years old when she was chosen to run 24 Winston Cup races for BAM Racing in 2002. "I have put in a lot of hard work over the years to develop consistency and to prove myself," Shawna says. "Now, finally, this opportunity has come." Team owner Beth Ann Morgenthau says, "Shawna is a splendid addition to the BAM Racing team. She has

Shawna's success at the Winston Cup level is showing that women can race well, too.

proven herself to be a very competitive NASCAR driver."

Shawna was born in Des Moines, Iowa, on November 30, 1964. No one thought that the little Robinson girl would grow up to become a race car driver. In fact, her first ride wasn't a car at all. Shawna made her racing debut in 1980 behind the wheel of a big-rig tractor in a Great American Truck Racing event.

She made the switch to stock cars in 1988, finishing third in her very first race at the Daytona International Speedway. Later that season she became the first woman to win a NASCAR Touring Series event. She won a "Dash" race in Asheville, North Carolina. Dash races are only about 150 miles (241 kilometers), but the racing action is just as furious. Capping off a great season, Shawna earned Dash Series Most Popular Driver and Rookie of the Year honors.

Shawna competed in four Busch Series events in 1991. The next year, after just 14 races, she was runner up in the division's Rookie of the Year standings. Then she took off several years to start a family with her husband, Jeff Clark. Jeff is also involved

with racing. He builds engines for Dale Earnhardt Jr.'s team.

In 2000, Shawna, then the mother of two, returned to the track. She competed in a full season of races in the top **ARCA** (American Race Car Association) stock car circuit, scoring top-10 finishes in nearly half her starts.

On June 10, 2001, Shawna became the first woman since 1989 to qualify for a Winston Cup event. She finished the Kmart 400 in Michigan in 34th place. She was the first female to complete a Winston Cup race since Janet Guthrie did it in 1980. Other female racers in the past included Patty Moise in 1989 and Robin McCall in 1982. Guthrie was mostly an Indy

Shawna got her start in "Dash" races, where the cars are smaller, but the action is just as fierce.

car driver. She entered a few Winston Cup events from 1976 through 1980.

After getting a taste of Winston Cup racing in 2001, Shawna remained determined to make it full-time. She got her chance when BAM signed her up.

"I've always wanted to compete," she says. "And if I compete, I want to win. I was born competitive, and that's in my blood. Whatever car I'm in, whatever series I'm running, whatever track I'm racing, I want to be in the hunt. I want people to know Shawna Robinson was there." Beginning in 2002, they all knew: She's a Winston Cup driver.

Shawna and BAM started 2002 with a bang when she qualified for the Daytona 500.

NOT FOR MEN ONLY

There haven't been too many
women drivers in NASCAR history, but those who have made it
are remarkable. That's certainly
the case with Janet Guthrie,
who was much more than a race
car driver.

Janet was born on March
7, 1938, in Iowa City, Iowa. She
earned her pilot's license when
she was 17. After graduating from the University of Michigan in 1960, she spent six
years working for an aviation company. During that time, she qualified for NASA's
astronaut training program.

Janet loved driving fast cars, too, and she started racing regularly in 1963.
She won several races on the Sports Car Club of America circuit. However, she
had bigger dreams. One was to drive in the Indianapolis 500. She tried out in 1976,
but didn't quite make it. That same year, however, Janet became the first woman to
compete in a Winston Cup race, finishing a respectable 16th in the Charlotte 600.
(Louise Smith raced in a Grand National race in 1949, before NASCAR changed the
name of the series to Winston Cup.)

In 1977, Janet did qualify at Indy and became the first woman to race in that
world-famous event. She had to drop out with mechanical problems, but a year
later finished ninth at Indy. Janet was inducted into the Women's Sports Hall of
Fame in 1980. Her selection was a just reward not only for her victories, but for her
hard work and never-give-up attitude.

The first great woman driver was Janet Guthrie, who
raced stock cars and Indy cars in the 1970s.

GLOSSARY

ARCA—stands for Automobile Racing Club of America, one of stock car racing's "minor leagues"

Busch Series—the top "minor league" circuit of NASCAR races. Busch is similar to baseball's Triple-A level.

checkered flag—black and white checked flag officials wave when the winner crosses the finish line

crew chief—person in charge of all of a race team's functions, especially on race day

go-kart—small, open-wheel racer specially made for young drivers

late model—a stock car that is no more than three years old

NASCAR—National Association for Stock Car Automobile Racing

race team—the owners, mechanics, and drivers who work together to buy, maintain, and race cars

ride—the term used for a job as a race car driver

stock car—a race car similar to factory-made automobiles sold by dealers to everyday drivers

Victory Lane—special area of a race track where winners go after a race to receive their prizes

Winston Cup Series—NASCAR's top circuit of races, for which drivers earn points toward an annual national championship

FOR MORE INFORMATION ABOUT NASCAR'S RISING STARS

Books

Center, Bill, and Bob Moore. *NASCAR: 50 Greatest Drivers*. New York: HarperHorizon, 1998.

Dale Earnhardt Jr.: Driving Force of a New Generation. Dallas: Beckett Publications, 2000.

Kirkpatrick, Rob. *Dale Earnhardt Jr.: NASCAR Power Racer*. New York: PowerKids Press, 2000.

Web Sites

The Official NASCAR Web Site
http://www.NASCAR.com
For an overview of an entire season of NASCAR as well as the history of the sport and a dictionary of racing terms

Dale Earnhardt Jr.
http://www.dalejr.com
Includes information about Dale's racing career and his famous family

Kevin Harvick's Official Web Site
http://www.kevinharvick.com
Read more about this hot young driver on his official Web site

Shawn Robinson's Official Web Site
http://www.shawnarobinson.com
NASCAR's top female driver talks about life on the track on her official site

INDEX

Atwood, Casey, 5, 19–24

Busch Series, 5, 6, 9, 10, 13–14, 15, 19, 20, 22, 26, 30

checkered flag, 8, 11, 15, 30
Childress, Richard, 9, 11, 17
Clark, Jeff, 27
Cracker Barrel 500, 9–10, 11
Craftsman Truck Series, 8–9, 20

Daytona 500, 16, 17, 24

Earnhardt, Dale, Jr. "Little E," 5, 11, 12–18, 27
Earnhardt, Dale, Sr. "The Intimidator," 5, 9, 11, 12, 16, 17, 18
Earnhardt, Kerry, 13, 16
Earnhardt, Ralph, 13, 15
Elliott, Bill, 24

Evernham, Ray, 24

France, William "Big Bill," 4, 25

go-kart, 7, 8, 19, 23, 30
Gordon, Jeff, 4, 11, 24
Guthrie, Janet, 27, 28, 29

Harvick, Kevin, 5, 6–11

Indianapolis 500, 28, 29

Jarrett, Dale, 4, 11
Johnson, Junior, 4

Late Model Stock Car division, 13, 20, 30
Linville, DeLana, 6

Marlin, Sterling, 18
McCall, Robin, 28
Moise, Patty, 28
Morgenthau, Beth Ann, 25

Nadeau, Jerry, 11

Pennzoil Freedom 400, 22, 24
Pepsi 400, 16, 17, 18
Petty, Richard, 4

Robinson, Shawna, 5, 25–29
Rudd, Ricky, 23

Smith, Louise, 29
Stewart, Tony, 24

Victory Lane, 5, 30

Waltrip, Michael, 16, 17, 18, 24
Winston Cup Series, 5, 6, 10, 11, 12, 15–16, 19, 22, 24, 25, 27, 28, 30
Women's Sports Hall of Fame, 29
World Karting Association, 19, 23

ABOUT THE AUTHOR

Bob Woods is a freelance writer in Madison, Connecticut. Over the past 27 years, his work has appeared in numerous magazines, including *Sports Illustrated, Newsweek International, Continental,* and *Chief Executive.* He has written sports biographies for young readers about Ken Griffey Jr., Barry Bonds, and Shaquille O'Neal.